M000033732

The Farm

Written by Claudia Logan

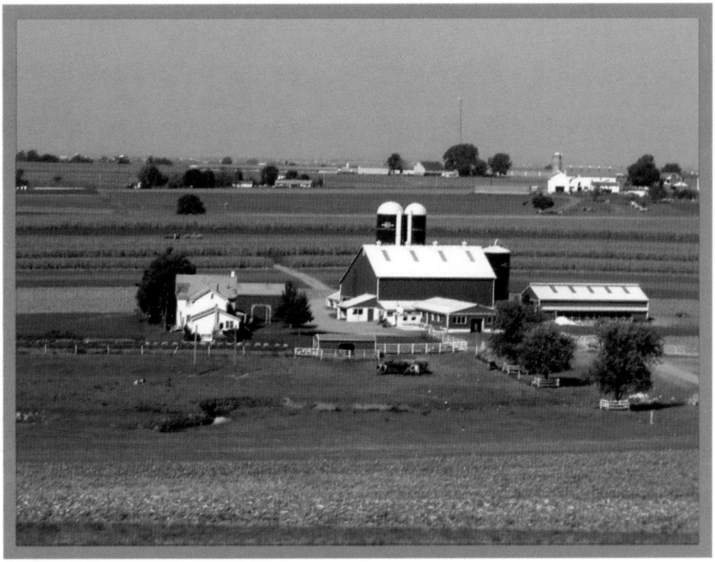

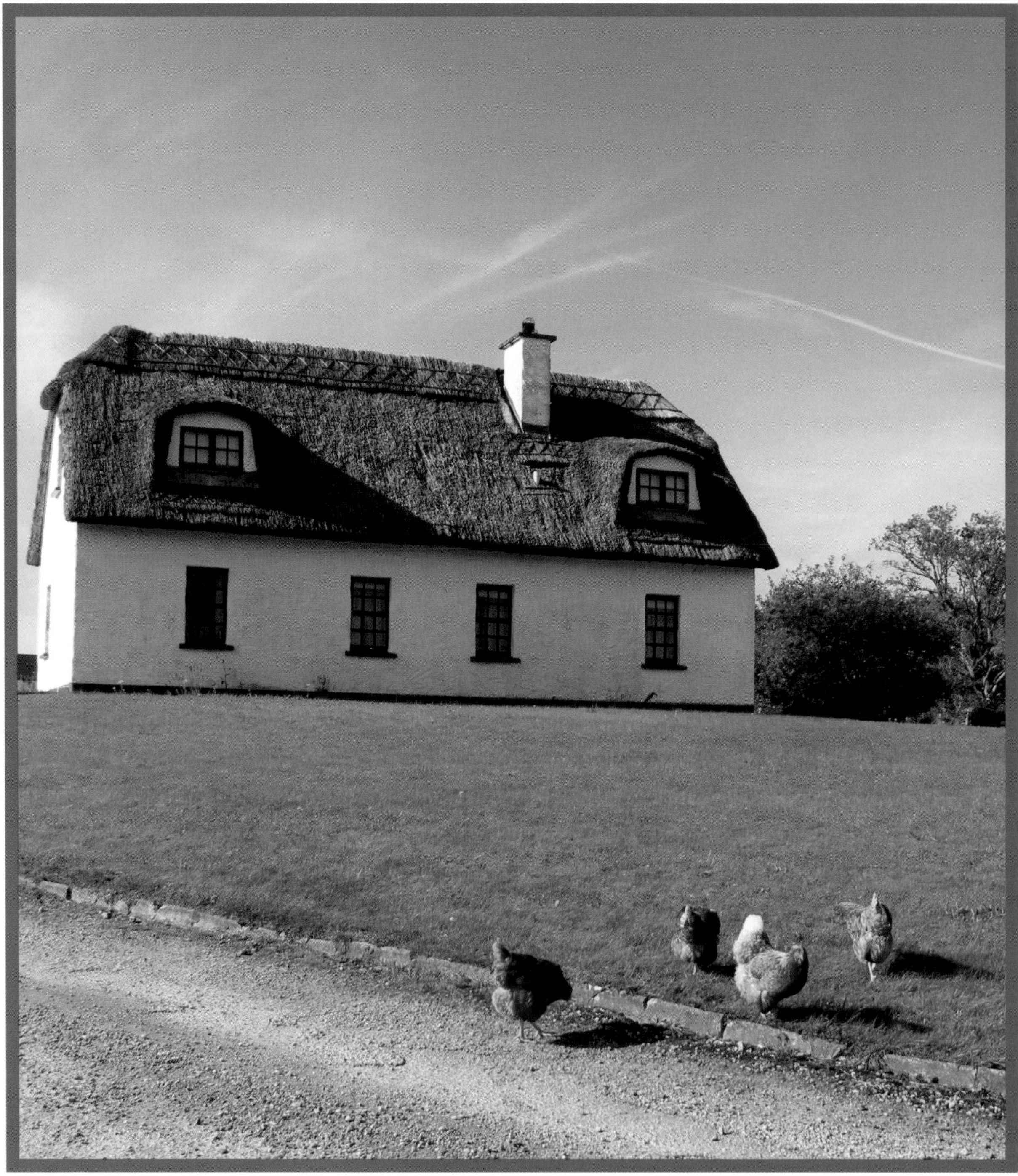

The house,

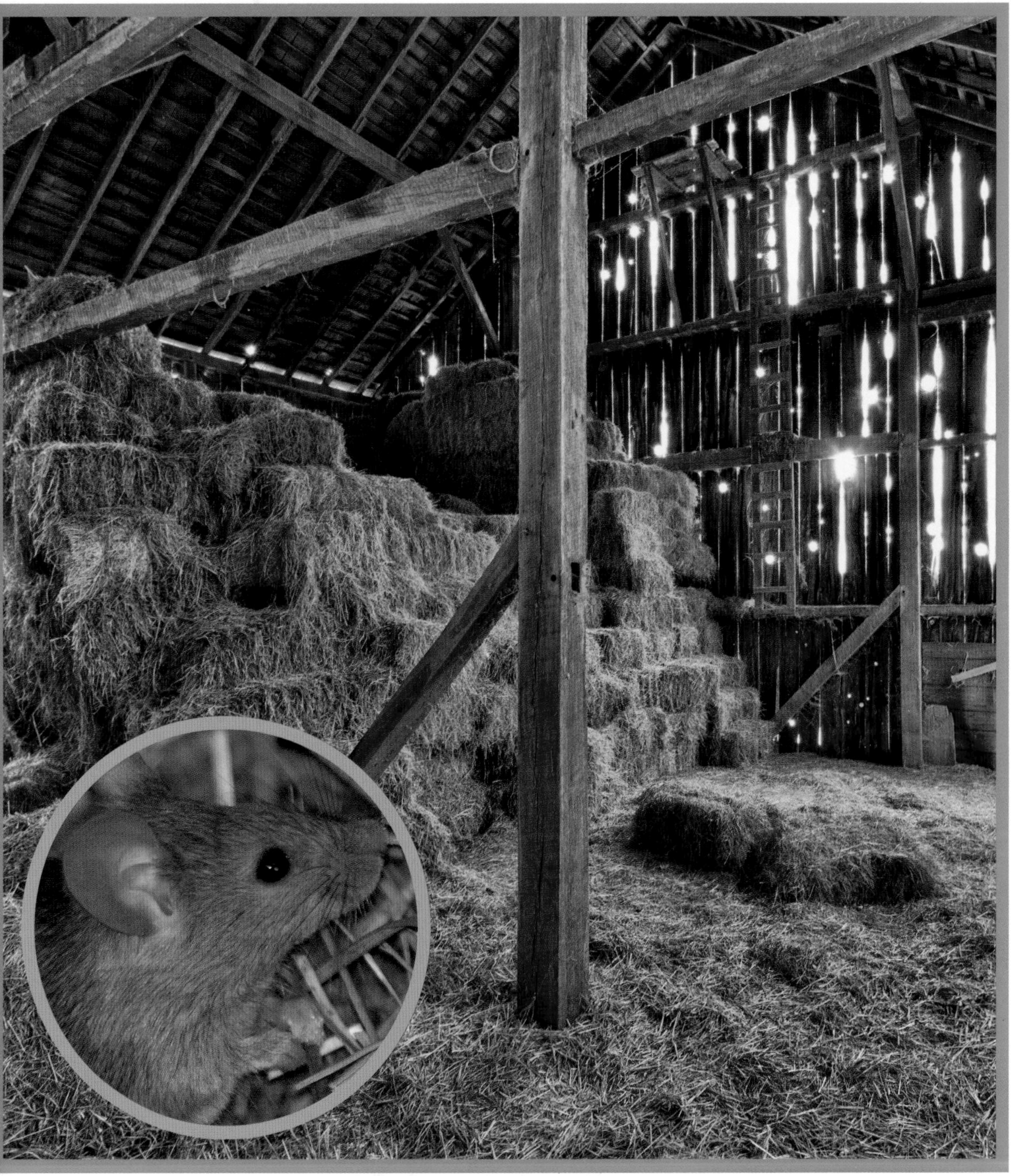

the mouse,

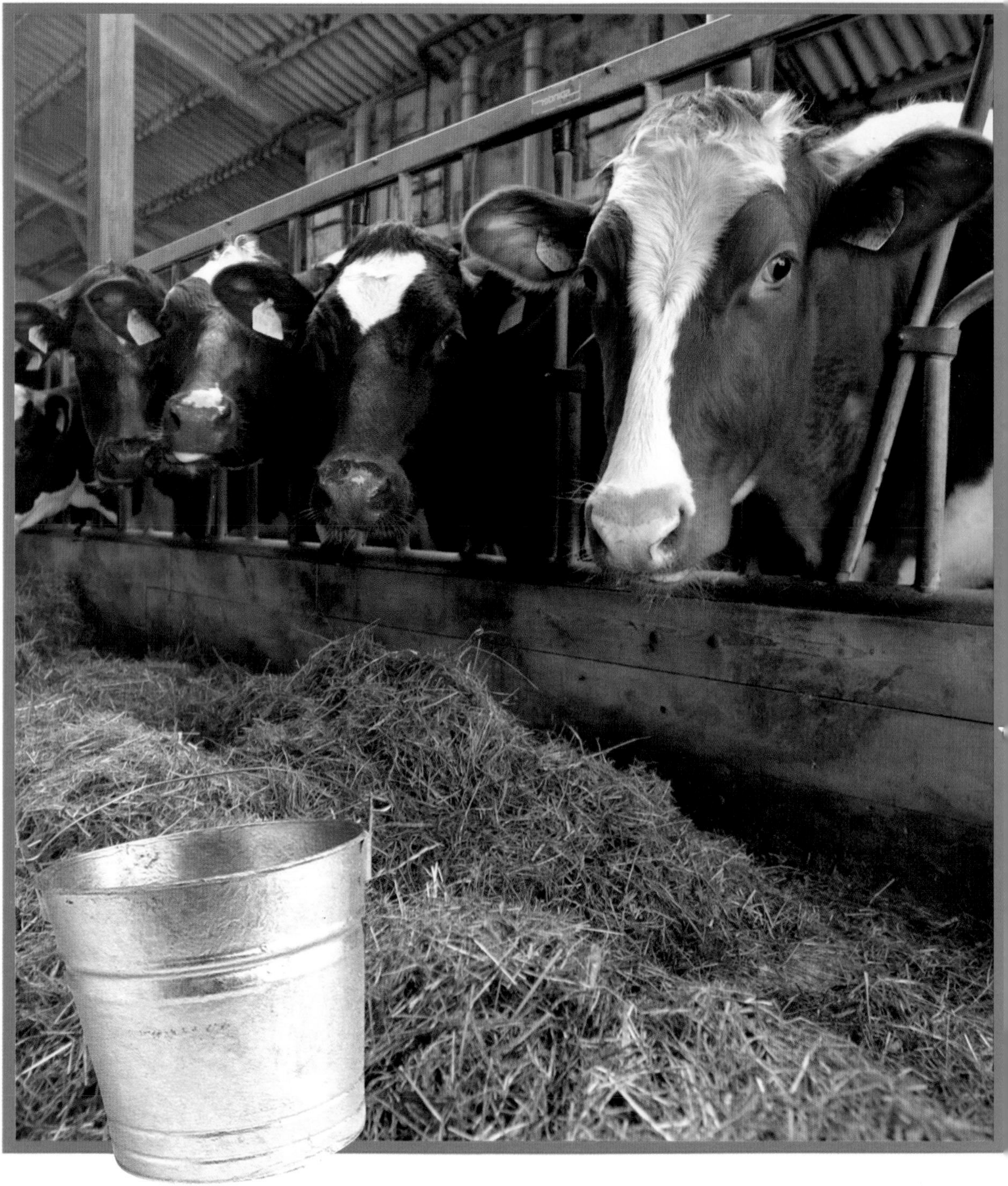

the pail,

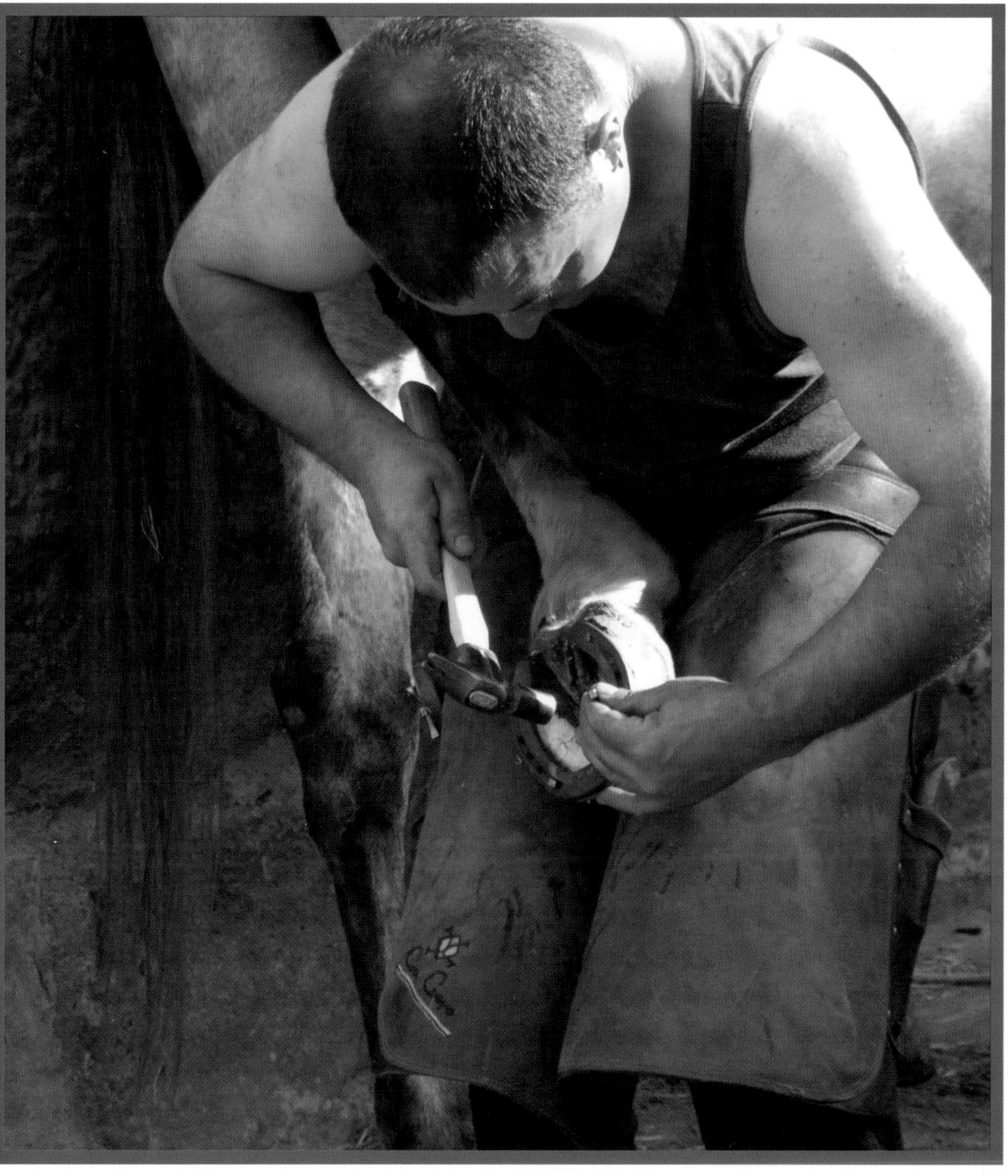

the nail,

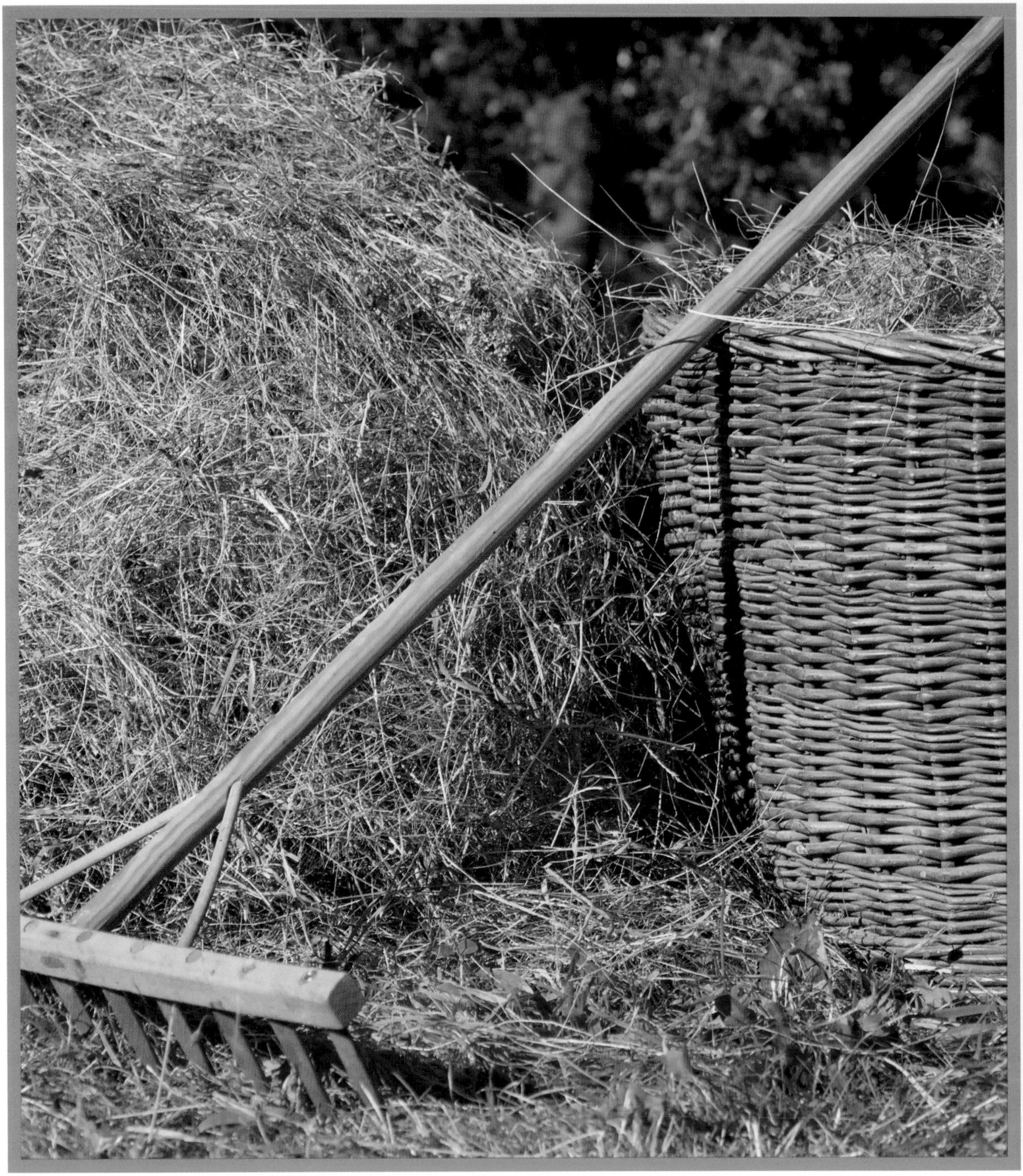

the rake,

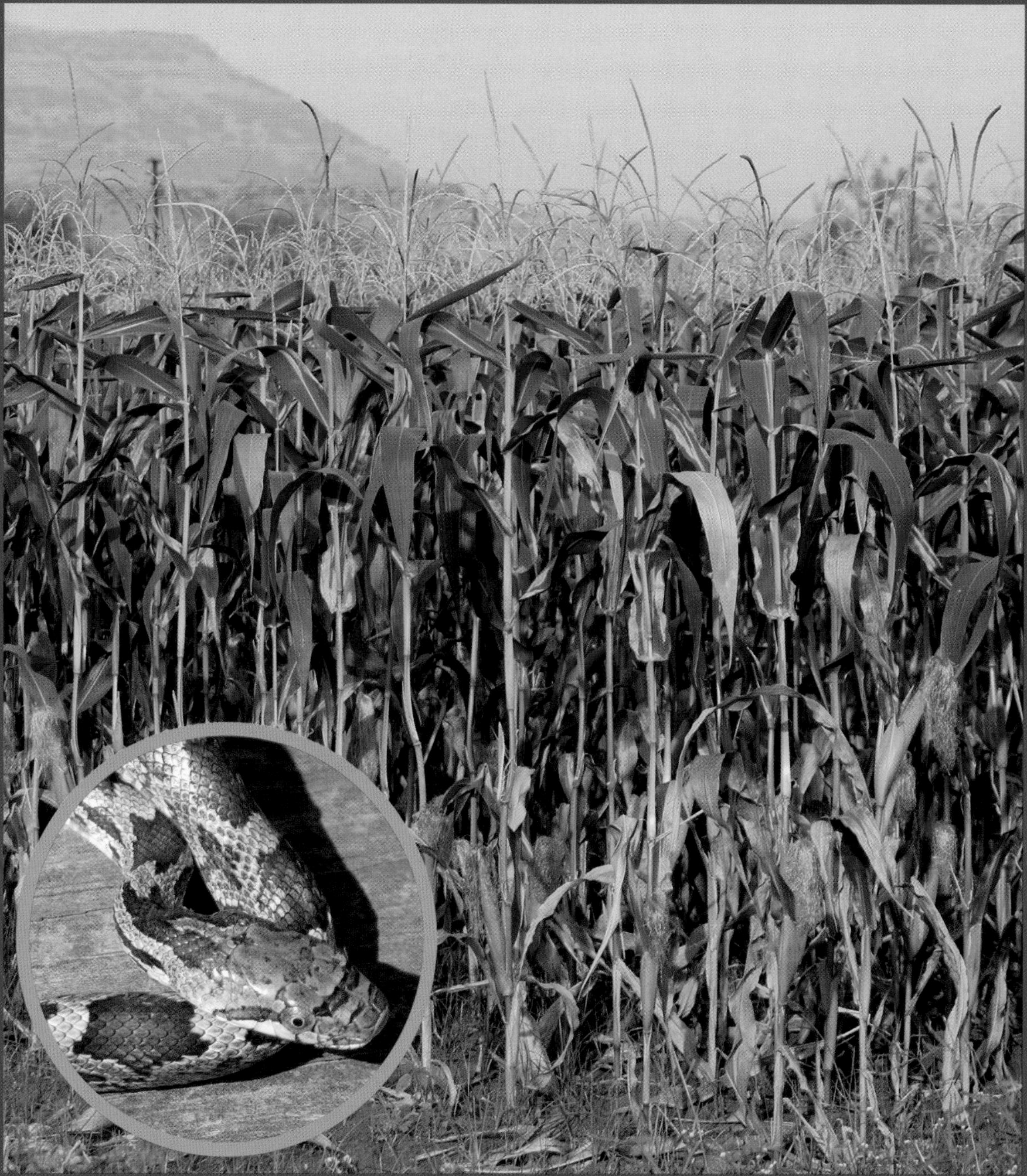

the snake,

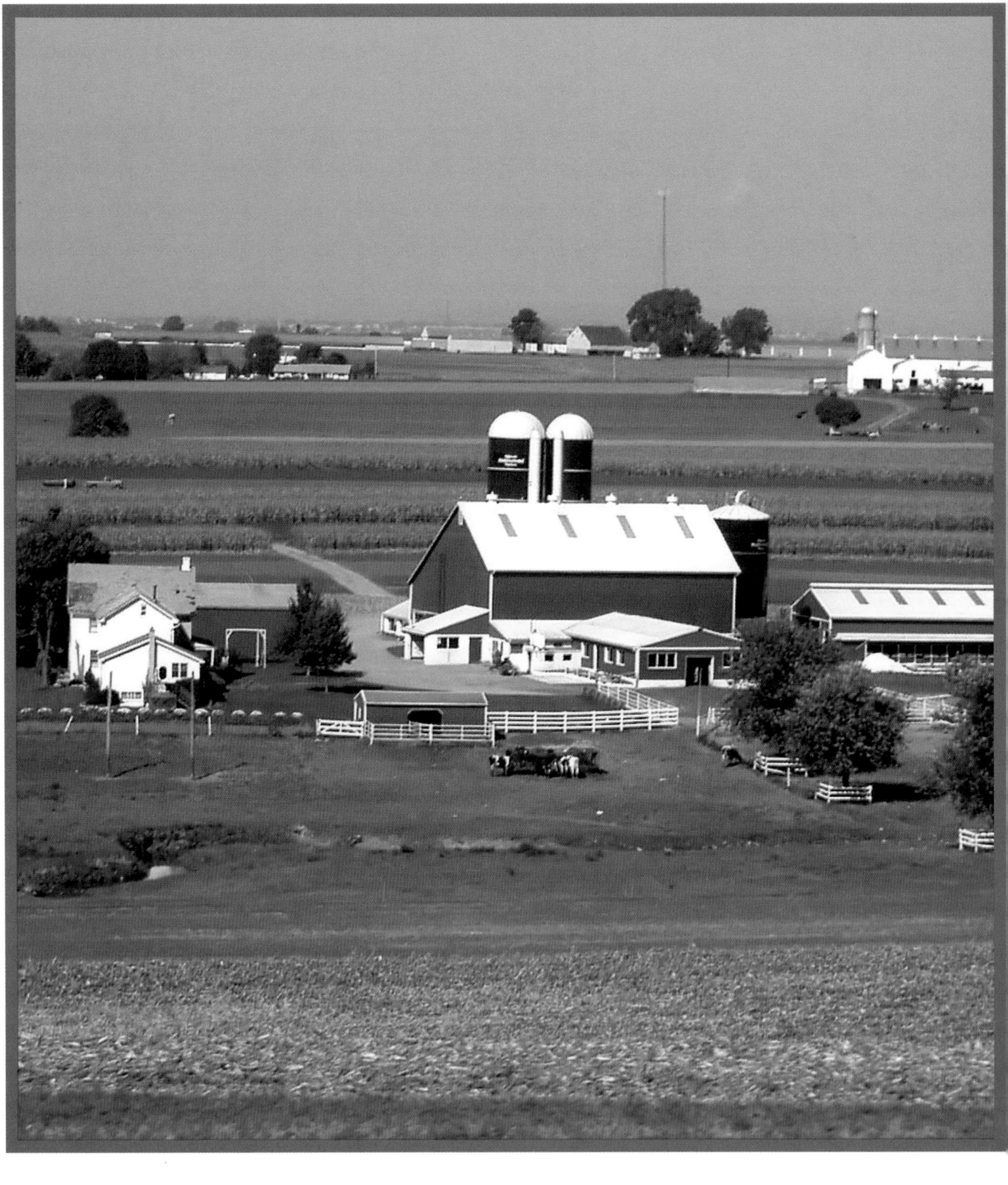

the farm.